just poems

E.S. Higgins

Copyright © 2022 Peanut Prints
All rights reserved.
ISBN: 978-0-6485460-4-7

Times I would come home and watch my mother cry

Back then when I was sleeping under a table I got wood chips in my eyes

I leant my dad some money and he walked towards the bottle shop

But then he remembered I was watching him and decided not

18 years old I was angry with the world

Confused and worked up over how my life would unfurl

I wandered alone for some time and read until my eyes would bleed

Dreaming of a world where my family would be financially free

But in years to come I realised I had no reason to complain

Beauty is an equal mix of both happiness and pain

And in youthful ignorance I cursed the world for what I thought it had done to me

Without any thought towards the people who really are in need

Now I find it hard to complain living by the beach

With loving friends and family within arm's reach

And slowly I began to understand that I'm as lucky as could be

Because at a young age I realised I had a dream

To follow relentlessly as the years would come

And even as I write this now the journey has barely begun

But, finally I'm starting to look forwards and not back

The day I realised that I needed to give thanks

For all the things that have made me, me

Far beyond the need to be financially free.

The borders of the city became like the fences of a farm.

I can see you there

Dancing in the light

Your face goes in and out of the shadows

There's only one beam of gold

A crack through a dark and quiet place

I can't even hear your footsteps.

And in the vast silence of it all you could still hear the groaning rusty air con units bolted to the outsides of the buildings.

The universe is made of waves

Life is made of waves

Heat, sound and light

All of them come in waves

And in the ocean waves crash against the shore

And when you ride a wave

The feeling is like nothing else

Because you're dancing with the universe

I woke up one day covered in dust

It was stuck to all the walls

It covered the streets and rushed passed me in the wind

I sat next to it on the bus

It was in the trains and in the cars

It was on my mirror when I tried to look into it

It was in the air

Floating through the universe

Caught up in an eternal wind

Carried here and there

Directionless and silent

One day I will turn to dust

If I haven't done so already

Blown away by the wind

Taken to a place where all the dust goes

Somewhere out there.

Working in the sun

There's brick dust in my lungs

When I'm crawling through roofs

Doing whatever the older boys tell me to do

They make me hate myself

So much that I want to be like them

A full-time bloke

A bunch of real men

Talking shit over some beers

Calling all my mates queers

I tried my best but I failed

Haunted by my shortcomings as a man

That's why I am the way I am

When my insecurities are on show

I guess now you know

That I would do all I can

To be a real man.

There I am in my room swiping away

Flicking through different faces but they all seem the same

My room is dark but the phone screen lights up my face

A notification pops up, I've run out of likes for today

I fall asleep and lose myself in dreams

Wake up in the morning but I still feel asleep

Drifting through the week like a butterfly caught in a breeze

I only feel free when I smoke weed

I guess deep down an escape is what I need

Everything is dark except my phone screen

I wonder what that means.

A bloke came to my market stall one Sunday

Shirtless and in boardies, He was covered in faded tats

His skin was leathery and his hair was grey and matted by salt

He hobbled on a broken toe

Black and blue in the sun

He asked me what the fuck I was doing

I told him poetry and he laughed and asked me for one

I wish I could remember what it was

And when I gave it to him he gave me 500 dollars

I refused but suddenly he grew serious

And told me he was the richest man in the world

And that he wanted to help me with my poems

And my publishing company peanut prints

He told me that it had taken him 6000 years to find me

I told him that I appreciated it, and politely refused his help

Before he left he asked me if I had a number for weed

I gave him mine and then he left

The next day he called my phone from an asylum

Someone ratted him in and four cops took him away

But he still wanted to help me

I was uneasy and he could tell

So he hung up, and I never heard from him again.

I often wonder if he was God.

We were smoking weed at age fourteen

Ordering two large pizzas under our parent's noses

Skating through ever street

L90 bus drivers our only chauffeurs

Back then we'd be out all day

Surfing or laying in some flowers

Days when we could do nothing at all

Play xbox all day or surf for hours

Days that are long gone and are only remembered from time to time

Distant memories lived in our minds.

Sick love

When you learn to be yourself again

Everything washes off of you like grime and dirt

You feel lighter

It feels as though you've just woken up from a heavy sleep

You were watching yourself on autopilot

Going to work and coming home

Constantly coming and going

Never staying anywhere too long

Waking up from time to time

Turning restlessly until you were comfy again

You wonder why it all happens the way it does

When you learn to be yourself again.

There are towers

That are squeezed so tight and so tall

That birds can't fly there anymore

Trapped in a birdcage

Just like me

There are bars of sunlight on the ground

I walk over them as I walk down the street

My skin prickles in the sunlight

On my way to work

Dancing in the sunlight

On the back of every wave

As water tumbles over

You turn to get out of the way

The wave crashes behind you

And covers you with spray

You close your eyes for a second

And for moment you try and feel your way

Water passes beneath you

Drawing up behind you like a mountain in the sea

The wind rushes through your hair

And for a few moments you feel free

You're descending

Your arms are up and you're flying down the face

You can hear your friends calling

But some feelings you could never say

The beauty of surfing could never be summarised

That was my attempt at trying to explain.

Fake news, fake information, fake people,

The tilt of a camera can make you look evil,

The click of a button can get you cancelled,

Banished forever for speaking your mind,

Although it's ok to be different,

As long as your differences are the same as mine,

Fake news, fake information, fake people,

Each day gets crazier than the next,

People against people,

Friends against friends,

I wonder if there will ever be truth,

Or if there will ever be an end,

Fake news, fake information, fake people.

Soft lights glow faintly through the rain like golden orbs

There's a car parked with its headlights on

A couple is in there laughing

In love and not wanting to get rained on

They make a mad dash for the front door

And scream with laughter as they run

But just before they go inside the man pulls her back

And kisses her in the rain.

You'll never find love if you go searching for it,

Love is too elusive for that,

You could never hope to lock love in a cage,

It would slip through all the gaps,

You could freeze love in a photo,

But in time those memories would make you sad,

And if you ever take love,

Then you should be prepared to give it back,

And love all things as they are,

That's the way love attracts.

What if you swipe right on the love of your life one day

You look at their pictures and think to yourself that they're the one

Maybe you've met them

They could already be gone

You could have passed them on the street

Without so much as a glance

Like a needle in a haystack

It all gets left to chance

You could lift up every stone and never find them

You could stand upon the tallest mountains and call out their names

And still get no closer

Silent moments soaked with pain

When you're looking out the window on the bus

Watching the hands tick over on your watch

Every moment further away

I hope that you find them one day.

The weeds that grow in the cracks of our minds

Whisper things we shouldn't hear

Foundations that are built upon foolish pride

Delusion when failure is near

Failure is a step towards learning

Lessons never spoken but felt inside

Failure cuts the weeds down

And brings out parts of us we try to hide

But still the weeds will regrow

They take over when the time is right

Until we fail again

And darkness turns to light.

Light reflected from the water shimmered through the glass and made waves on the ceiling of the boat

The sea was glimmering in the sunlight

It felt like a dream

Everything looked as if it were a part of some heavenly painting

Splashed against the walls of some ancient temple

Half asleep I stumbled off the boat

Sweating my brains out

I felt like puking but it wasn't because of the boat ride

I was up all night staring at neon lights In dimly lit places

Under ground where everyone yells

I winced in the sunlight

And shuffled home hollow and broken

I tell myself it's the last time

But I know I'm lying.

When you fall in love again

You never thought that it would happen

Years of silence suddenly filled with music

Your walls crumble down around you

And although you've tasted the bitter pain

That comes after a deafening heartbreak

You'd do it all again

Just to fall in love again.

In the thundering rain

I look out the window

It's covered in droplets that form little rivers that crawl down the glass

The trees are dancing in the wind

I wonder what the birds are doing.

You feel as though you are better without

And each day your mind fills you with doubt

About who you are and where you are going

When you get lost along the way and fear growing

Sometimes I wonder if I'm still asleep

Drifting through life I need

To wake myself up but I'm not sure how

I guess the thought is ok for now.

Floating in the darkness

My memories are like windows in a storm

I press my face against the glass and peer through

The light hurts my eyes for a moment

It looks warm inside

There are blue skies and clear water

Diving under crashing waves

I can see myself gliding

Carelessly and effortlessly

And for a moment I forget where I am

And re live my youth one last time.

I wonder what he thinks about

At night when he's alone

Or in the engine rooms that he works in underground

Groaning and churning

Eating up all the silence

I wonder what he thinks about

At night when he's alone

Listening to laughter on the street

Party goers on their way home

He was never one for parties

The loud noise made him feel sick

Long nights full of loneliness

Softened with hard drink

I wonder who he was thinking about

All those years in silence

Remembered only by him

At night when he is alone.

An old boy in high viz and a faded cap

Sits alone by the pub window

Watching the people outside pass by

He hates most things

Except for his missus and his kids

Or listening to old school rock and roll

And a cold schooner after a hard day's work.

In the Caribbean sun

The sound of parang was playing from the kitchen

While granny was cooking stew chicken

I was just a boy

Old enough to remember

But too young to really appreciate it all

The little smells and sounds

That form the backbone of your being.

In some dark and windy storm
I nearly lost my life

I paddled out and snapped my board

And no one could hear my cries

I got sent below

Tossed and ripped apart by mountain waves

I lost all of my air

And realised that this would be the day

But I grabbed onto a rock shelf

And was pushed into the cliff where I was safe

I clambered up

And threw up all over the cliff face

I wobbled back to the sand

Tears masked by sea spray

And hugged my brother

I'll never forget that day.

When you fall in love suddenly you can't say the right words

And everything you do seems foolish and embarrassing

You lose your cool

And everything you feel inside is desperate and volatile

When you fall in love you look at yourself

High up somewhere and scared to fall

You try and rub the kisses off your cheek

To convince yourself that it's not real

But they won't rub away.

Promises forgotten

Made up by children long ago

Sworn by heart

Deep down everyone knows

The dreams that were left

Somewhere in the out land

Made of colours and songs

We could no longer understand

I wish I could go there again

Even just for a day

To see who I was

And who I became along the way

If I was there I would listen

To all those things I forgot

Lessons on how to be a child again

In a world that forgot.

He fell to his knees laughing, but a moment later he burst into tears.

The little boy put his hand on the man's shoulder and asked him what was wrong.

In a choking splutter through laughter and tears the man smiled and said that it was something adults did sometimes.

The little boy nodded. He was satisfied with the answer and didn't ask again.

He sat back and watched the man for a time, but then he got bored and ran off to play again.

When he returned the man was gone.

Things you didn't understand as a child

Reveal themselves with age

Pure moments made of happiness and sadness

Reflecting on times that are long gone

You peer through the looking glass of your memories

At a toothless grin with grazed knees

Out in the sun somewhere

Far away where your fears can't find them.

Pain masked by laughter

You can see it in their eyes

Mouths wide open

Are open just the same when they cry

Positive in nature

But it only takes a nudge to break

Why are you putting on a brave face?

You know its ok to cry

Nobody's gonna judge you

If it makes you feel better I'll cry too

As long as you let it all go

All that weight will flush away

Like a cloud that's carrying too much rain

Let it all go and float away

Even though it may scare you

Most things worth it are

Then when you laugh again you'll feel alive

Instead of trying to hide

Tears that are gonna fall one day anyways

Why are you trying to be brave?

Her beauty made me feel like a weird creature

One with awkward arms and legs

Everything I said made me cringe on the inside

But she smiled like the sun

While we sat on the floor of her living room and listened to music

I put my arm around her

And my body language said what my words couldn't

As we melted into one another

I laughed in disbelief.

The in-between moments

Full of silence

While you watch the world go by

And listen to the sounds

Of different people who are all like you

Passing by for a short moment

On their way somewhere

Different to you but still the same

That's what makes it special.

When your heart is hurting

You can hear the music of life

Sweet but sad

Because it is only temporary

You drink it in

Until your heart is full

Of memories that make you laugh and weep.

There is a garden full of hearts somewhere

That beat to the rhythm of bird songs

In a place where the light is always cool and golden

The shadows are long and the trees sway back and forth gently

Before the gardener comes and picks out all the ripe ones.

I never wanted to grow up

I used to sleep in a little ball so I wouldn't grow

And on the night before my thirteenth birthday I made a promise to myself

That I would never let go of my childhood soul.

I was dating girls and never seemed to be interested in any

I got my heart broken and I was worried I'd never have that feeling of love again

I talked to one of the boys on site

He was a fighter and covered in tattoos

He told me something simple and beautiful

That if you meet someone, and then don't like the idea of not spending more time with them

And if you miss them even though you haven't known them long

They're probably the one.

What if you couldn't hear a thing?

If all of a sudden, the world was bathed in silence

You try to yell and scream

But nothing comes out

At first, you're scared and confused

All you can feel is the beating of people's hearts

Rippling through the air

Like one collective pulse

That connects all life

Like a beating drum

Would things change?

The meaning of life is understood by children

But they have no words to describe it

So, it is lost.

"What is love?" The Caterpillar asked the Mockingbird one afternoon atop the tree they shared,
"Love is the wind against your face and the open skies at your reach. Come I shall show you" it replied and then flew away,
But the Caterpillar could not fly after it, for it was landlocked without the wings the Mockingbird had been blessed with,
And soon the Mockingbird had disappeared completely leaving the Caterpillar alone atop the tree,
As it peered up longingly at the open sky it came to a conclusion,
"Love is selfish".

The next morning the Caterpillar met a lone Ant who was making its way down the tree with a crumb almost twice his size hoisted on his back,
"What is love?" The Caterpillar asked it as it passed by,
The Ant lifted its head, straining from the burden of the crumb on its back and replied,
"Love is duty, to work and protect the ones you care about",
As it crawled off once more the Caterpillar said to

itself with a scoff,
"Love is tedious".

That very afternoon whilst the Caterpillar was snacking on some leaves it spotted a Squirrel banging an acorn against the trunk of the tree,
The Caterpillar, curiously watching the Squirrel work away at the acorn posed to it the very same question, "What is love?"
The squirrel looked up from its task, tilting its head and said "Love is the thing that lays hidden within something",
Finally, the acorn cracked open and the Squirrel dashed away to feed its family,
As the Caterpillar watched the Squirrel dart off it saw that although the acorn it carried meant nothing to the Caterpillar, it was the duty the Squirrel held as a means of feeding and protecting its family,
The breaking of the acorn was tedious,
But what was inside meant the prosperity for the ones it loved,
As the Caterpillar sat and watched it whispered to itself,
"love is beautiful".

That night the Caterpillar wrapped itself up in a tight cocoon,
For the day had been long and it needed rest,
And the very next morning the most beautiful of butterflies arose in its place,
With a single flap of its golden wings, it took to the open skies where it let the radiance of the sun wash over its new body,
And as it floated away in the soft breeze it looked down at the tree that had once been its home and said,
"Love is freedom".

Most poetry can't be written or said

It's in the yawning silence between words

When you're looking out into the horizon

It's in getting older and realising that you know nothing at all

Or much less than you thought you did anyway

It's in the moments when you smile to yourself

Or at someone you love when they're not looking

Those moments can't be put into words properly

And if you try to it won't do it justice

Poetry is silence.

To think that everyone around me came from a ballsack..

Back then in days of sunlight

That used to turn our hair golden

My friends and I would be in the water all day

And afterwards we'd get milkshakes

At night, we'd share warm beers

Stolen from our parent's cupboards

Three shit beers between three shit kids

Laughing in the darkness just out of view from the street lights.

You wonder what they're up to

Now that your worlds are split apart

You think of looking them up

But the thought brings pain

You wonder most of all

If they still think about you too

You tell yourself that they don't

But in your heart, you know that they do.

People are cheering

They're laughing and enjoying themselves

The sound makes you smile

Even though they're in the distance

You know how it would feel to be there

Surrounded by friends and family.

You turn your face away

From the suns light

That reveals the imperfections on your face

Worried over people's glances

Every dart of the eye is like a strike against your being

You stoop your head low

And sink into the background

Hoping not to be noticed

You wish you were like them.

The sun doesn't exist without us.

If there were no planets in the solar system

No moons or asteroids floating about in space

Where would the suns light go?

Swallowed up by the never-ending darkness

When the sunlight hits our faces

We smile and feel alive

And so too does the sun.

How could we live in cities full of people

Crammed together in buses and trains

And still feel alone?

When you watch your memories again

Now that you're older and have learned many lessons

Things begin to make sense

Why you are the way you are

You are the sum of your parent's biggest achievements

And also, their greatest mistakes.

Aye haven't seen you in ages cunt how you been?

Me?

I been good, keeping out of trouble and that

Actually, just got back from a trip to Thailand

Me and the boys were out there running amuck

Bro you ever heard of 6 cunts spending 6 grand to go somewhere just to fuck?

Was hectic but it was almost too much

Prolly get a missus soon with some luck

Been working heaps, like 6 days a week

Shits fucked how you gotta work your whole life just to eat

Breath in brick dust all day while I fuck up both my knees

I reckon I'll get rich one day on the pokies but I guess we'll see

Anyways bro was good to see you lets catch up in the week.

Most people know how

Some people know why

One in a million understand.

I remember as a boy

I stood over my dad while he was sleeping at the computer

I looked at his hands

He had hair on his knuckles

I smiled to myself

And even though I never wanted to grow up

I smiled because I knew at least I would grow up to be like him.

I was eleven years old living in the middle east

Riding around alone on my bike

There was no grass along the pavement

Just dirt and sand

I remember at Ramadan

There were goats tied outside of people's houses

I used to try and pet them

But one day they disappeared

I was old enough to know why.

I bought a toy AK-47 from the corner shop outside the mosque

I slung it around my back as I rode my bike

Until I found a little mound of sand

Where I would lay down and pretend to have a shoot out

The gun would light up and make noises

I got up and brushed the dirt off of my clothes

Blew the hair from my eyes

And rode off down the street.

Driving down the highway with my dad

The desert stretched out into the horizon

While we blasted Amy Winehouse

And changed the words from chasing pavement

To chasing penguins

The last time we were together for a long period of time

Memories I'll take with me for the rest of my life.

When you leave somewhere for the last time

And you know you'll never be back

You close your eyes for a moment before you go

And try to freeze time

Everything seems different

A chapter that's closing before your eyes

Visited again only in your memories.

What could you say of a broken heart

That opens itself up again despite being scarred

And even though it fell so far

Its willing to climb back up to the start

And although its much heavier now

It's a testament to the sounds

Of laughter and music

Both can open the door to the soul

And drown out the silence that can swallow us whole

What could you say then of a broken heart?

Knowing that one day it will find its way back to the start

And love again.

Time is just a construct

Back then we are still alive

Existing forever

In those times

That you look back on when things are going bad

You can visit them whenever
You're happy or sad

They will never change

Like chapters of a book we can open again

Life has no real beginning or end

Only memories.

One little crack doesn't mean that its broken

And if your insecurities are seeping through then you should be open

Because if you can listen to them

And have the strength to tell them that they're wrong

You realise that there was nothing to fear all along

Most of those things are in your head

Swimming through the darkness while you're lying in bed

Convincing you that you're not worth anything at all

And scaring you when you rise into believing that you'll fall

And maybe one day that might be true

But happiness and sadness are just as important for you

In shaping you into everything you could be

Regardless of your insecurities.

The music of nature

Plays wherever you go

It rises and falls like a symphony

And echoes when you are alone

Staring out into the horizon

Your heart forms a drumbeat

That beats with the universe

Music is poetry.

Dreams extinguished by years of pain

Memories lost within flooding rains

Slipped through our fingers we travel forwards and back

Life is a pathway but we always lose track

But no great story ends without getting lost

No great wins come without great loss

As long as you keep your feet planted firmly on the road

There's no telling the places you'll go.

Freckles upon a face

Scrunched up in the sunlight

By the hundreds and thousands

Reminders of happy days and sunshine

Freckles upon the face

Of someone that you love

The little things about them

All the quirks and weird stuff

Freckles upon a face

Always seem to make me smile

Freckles upon a face

Memories of being a child.

just poems

E.S. Higgins

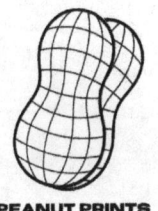

**PEANUT PRINTS**

www.ingramcontent.com/pod-product-compliance
Lightning Source LLC
Chambersburg PA
CBHW010707020526
44107CB00082B/2707

# THE BOOK OF QUESTIONS

## Living with Chronic Illness

Brianna Greenspan
Gregory Stock, PhD

Copyright © 2025 Gregory Stock and Brianna Greenspan
All rights reserved. No portion of this book may be reproduced—mechanically, electronically, or by any other means, including photocopying—without written permission of the publisher.

Library of Congress Cataloging-in-Publication Data is available.

Paperback ISBN: 978-0-9862092-5-3
Ebook ISBN: 978-0-9862092-6-0

Nquire Media
nquiremedia.com

Printed in the United States of America
First Printing August 2025

10 9 8 7 6 5 4 3 2 1

Print cover and interior design by G Sharp Design, LLC

"After 15 years of helping families and children impacted by chronic illness, I have learned there is a great need to be seen and connect with others. This book is an amazing tool to overcome isolation and engage in processing all aspects of challenging health issues."

—PHYLLIS BEDFORD, Lyme disease advocate, co-founder and executive director of LymeLight Foundation

"Stock and Greenspan have created an invaluable tool that helps those facing chronic illness find their voice, connect authentically, and uncover unexpected meaning in their journeys. Profoundly powerful."

—SCOTT SIMON, speaker, author, experience designer, and founder & CEO of Scare Your Soul

"As a chronic disease researcher and as someone whose family has been shaped by the realities of lifelong health conditions, this book struck a deep chord with me. *The Book of Questions: Living with Chronic Illness* is both a practical tool and an emotional lifeline. Dr. Stock's signature approach to life's most challenging and thought-provoking questions is on full display in this book, revealing the depth of his wisdom and insight, now beautifully expanded through Brianna Greenspan's lived experience. Together, they've created something rare: a gentle, powerful companion for anyone learning to live and love through the uncertainty of illness."

—SAVI GLOWE, researcher, advocate, and founder of BioAstra, Inc.

"When faced with the impossible, a new version of ourselves emerges. *The Book of Questions: Living with Chronic Illness* encourages us to explore our identity outside of pain, offering a beautiful journey of acknowledgment, healing, and living fully. It's a must-read for the chronic illness community."

—**NIKITA WILLIAMS**, top-rated podcast host and award-winning business coach

"In *The Book of Questions: Living with Chronic Illness*, Stock and Greenspan create a rare gift of questions that are profound and illuminating. They offer the opportunity to examine deep truths about living and what it means and feels to be human."

—**DON PONTURO**, Former Director of Communications, UCLA Department of Pediatrics, UCLA Mattel Children's Hospital

"As someone who has witnessed and celebrated healing through food and positivity, *The Book of Questions: Living with Chronic Illness* feels like a true soul-sister companion on the journey to awakening. Powerful and needed."

—**GABRIELLE REYES**, award-winning singer, actress, musical chef, cookbook author, and TV host

"This compassionate guide offers individuals living with chronic illness a pathway to their inner wisdom and resilience—reminding us that even in difficulty, profound well-being remains possible."

—**CYNTHIA WHITAKER**, PsyD, President & CEO, Greater Nashua Mental Health

**PRAISE FOR**
***THE BOOK OF QUESTIONS: LIVING WITH CHRONIC ILLNESS***

"*The Book of Questions: Living with Chronic Illness* is a powerful and compassionate guide that gives voice to the silent struggles so many endure. It doesn't offer prescriptions—it offers something even more essential: the right questions. These questions invite reflection, connection, and healing, helping us shift from powerlessness to possibility. As a physician who's spent decades helping people reclaim their health, I've learned that transformation begins not with answers, but with the courage to ask better questions. This book is a lifeline for anyone navigating the invisible terrain of chronic illness."

—**MARK HYMAN**, MD, *New York Times* bestselling author of *Young Forever* and host of The Dr. Hyman Show

"Stock and Greenspan remind us of something powerful and essential: it is the questions we choose to ask that can profoundly alter our experience with chronic illness."

—**VIVEK H. MURTHY**, MD, MBA, 19th and 21st Surgeon General of the United States

"Chronic illness is—or will be—a part of everyone's life in the United States. Most of us will live with at least one chronic illness in our lifetime and all of us will be close to people who live with them. In *The Book of Questions: Living with Chronic Illness*, Greenspan and Stock give us an essential set of tools to navigate these challenges—probing questions that help us gain perspective, reflect, and find paths forward."

—**STEPHEN J. DOWNS**, Co-Founder, Building H, and Former Chief Technology and Strategy Officer, Robert Wood Johnson Foundation

"As an Alzheimer's advocate, I frequently speak to those recently diagnosed with Alzheimer's who are experiencing despair about having less time than they expected. For many, however, their question soon becomes, 'How can I find greater joy out of each day I do have with my family?' The more successful the answer to that question, the greater their happiness."

—**GEORGE VRADENBURG,** Co-Founder and Chairman, UsAgainstAlzheimer's

"In *The Book of Questions: Living with Chronic Illness*, Stock and Greenspan shine a light of clarity into the complexity of managing health issues. By prompting insightful conversations (and thoughts) through questioning, this life-changing book helps us honor our values, spark our resilience, and pave the path to a hopeful, meaningful life."

—**JENNIFER CRAMER-MILLER,** wellness advocate and author of *Incurable Optimist: Living with Illness and Chronic Hope*

"This book's masterful questions and format serve as a unique gift, providing both comfort and inspiration. It is rare to encounter a work that resonates so deeply, and your book is undoubtedly one of them. Thank you for your remarkable contribution; it is a powerful and helpful learning tool and resource!"

—**KARL ROBB,** Parkinson's Disease advocate, blogger, and author of *A Soft Voice in a Noisy World: A Guide to Dealing and Healing with Parkinson's Disease*

"For many living with chronic illness, the epidemic of loneliness is often the most consuming and painful part of the journey. This book offers a plausible antidote—a compassionate and thoughtfully crafted guide to help transform isolation into connection through the simple yet profound and meaningful art of questioning."

—**KRIS ARMSTRONG,** speech language pathologist, certified brain injury specialist, caregiver of a loved one for more than 15 years, and storyteller

"As a physician for over 40 years, I've witnessed firsthand the profound impact chronic illness has on individuals and their families. The questions in this book are pure gold—creating pathways for understanding and healing that both patients and caregivers desperately need."

—**DAN DIAMOND,** MD, family physician and award-winning educator

"For two decades, Greg Stock's questions have been my secret tool—for sparking fresh conversations, stirring up old ones, energizing teams, and revealing me to myself."

—**RACHEL BELLOW,** Founder & Executive Board Chair, Bonfire Women, Inc.

"These questions challenge anyone who's willing to look directly at what it means to live inside a body, to need others, and to keep showing up anyway. A rare and generous offering."

—**ERIN BURGOON,** PhD, author of *Joyful A-F: The Essential Business Strategy*

"Through thoughtful and empowering prompts, Brianna Greenspan and Dr. Gregory Stock invite you to dig deep, honor your journey, and reclaim your voice. This book is more than a guide—it's a beacon of resilience, clarity, and connection for anyone navigating life with chronic illness."

—**DR. JILL KAHN**, author of *The Gift of Taking*, founder of The BioCode System®, and coauthor of the Everything Is Right About You series

"The most powerful questions don't demand answers—they invite us to pause, get curious, and choose a path forward with greater self-compassion. This book does just that. It gently opens space for those living with chronic illness to be seen, heard, and reconnected to their own resilience and wisdom—one question at a time."

—**MAUREEN (MO) MCKENNA**, Eclectic Explorer, Return on Energy

"As someone who has walked alongside loved ones facing the daily realities of chronic illness—as a caregiver, family member, and parent—I know the quiet ache of wanting to help but not always knowing how. *The Book of Questions: Living with Chronic Illness* offers a gentle, profound way in. These questions aren't just words on a page—they are invitations to connect, to understand, and to heal. This book is a compassionate companion for anyone navigating the weight of illness, reminding us that even in the hardest moments, hope, resilience, and love can still lead the way."

—**CAROLYN COLLEEN BOSTRACK**, PhD, author, speaker, executive leader, and humanitarian

## TO MOM AND DAD,

*for all that you have done and continue to do for me. I am who I am because of you both. I love you endlessly.*
—*Brianna*

## TO SPIKE CARLSON,

*whose courage in facing degenerative disease and blindness when I was his student was deeply inspiring.*
—*Greg*

# INTRODUCTION

**QUESTIONING AS A PATH TO HEALING**

I (Brianna) still recall my first experience with a powerful question. It was March 6, 2008. I was a sophomore in college, getting ready to see the surgeon who'd recently performed the spinal fusion that was supposed to relieve me of the pain that had been torturing me for the past eight years.

I asked myself, *If this excruciating pain never went away, would I even want to live anymore?* And my answer was no.

I'd always had health issues. As a baby, I cried constantly, until I learned to talk—and then I complained constantly about the pain, infections, insomnia, allergic reactions, stomach problems, and skin conditions I experienced daily.

I would frequently throw up before school, on the way to school, or at school. Every morning, I fought with my mom about eating breakfast—she wanted to make sure I was nourished for the day, when I knew I couldn't hold it down—my body kept telling me no, no, no! I assumed everyone missed school regularly for doctor's appointments. It was just the way life was.

Then, at age eleven, I began experiencing severe back pain—on top of all my other symptoms. The pain was intense and unceasing, and every step was excruciating. I'd still throw up several times a day, often without warning, but now throwing up escalated my pain from a 6 to a 9, which could not be relieved by the ever-growing cocktail of medications and painkillers I was taking.

After eight years of specialist appointments, assistive devices, diagnoses, medications, labels, and therapies, there were more challenges than ever, but no solutions.

And then there was a ray of hope. I was told that I needed spinal surgery, an L5-S1 fusion, and there was a good chance it would get rid of my back pain for good. *Sign me up!* I thought. There was so much hope, relief, and even excitement leading up to the surgery—not just for myself, but for those around me.

I had the surgery the summer before my sophomore year of college. The moment I woke up, I knew something was wrong. The pain was ten times what it had been before the surgery. It didn't just hurt to walk. Everything hurt. It hurt to move. It hurt to breathe. It hurt to exist.

Daily life became unimaginably excruciating. My friends drove me to school, we parked in a handicapped spot, and someone met me there and took me to class on a golf cart. Even while drugged on painkillers, every pothole was painful. I wore the back brace, did the physical therapy, got the steroid shots, took the medications—but the increased pain remained. My doctors told me I just needed to work harder.

This was not the life I wanted.

So, on the morning of March 6, 2008, the day of my follow-up appointment to get an official assessment of the surgery, I believed it was my fault I was still in pain. I had been 100 percent sure the procedure would work—but what if it hadn't?

That's when I asked myself whether I even wanted to live in such pain. And just as I decided I didn't, the phone rang. It was my college roommate, calling to tell me that my best friend, whom I had seen twelve hours earlier, had just overdosed on a high-level painkiller and died.

WHAT? He was no junkie; just a kid experimenting after a very hard day. After three hours of grappling with the shock and confusion, my parents led me to the car to see my surgeon. When we got there, I was told the surgery had failed, and until they could figure out what to do next, they suggested taking . . . the same painkiller my friend had died from.

"Wait," I said, bewildered. "That drug just killed my best friend. Couldn't it kill me?"

"You just told us that it hurts to move, you're suffering, and it's the worst it's ever been," the surgeon answered. "You need this medication. It will help you until we can find a better solution."

And that's when it hit me: the scenario I had feared this morning was actually happening. The best that doctors could offer was a drug that had just killed my best friend. They had nothing else. This pain really might NEVER go away.

But instead of wanting to end my life, a different question came to me: *Is there anything else out there that can help me with what I'm currently experiencing—and if so, where can I find it?*

That was the moment of my awakening. That was the shattering, painful miracle that launched my journey of asking questions with the intention of growth and healing.

My first question was unintentional. I just wanted the pain to go away; I didn't really want to end my life. Just like my best friend's tragic passing was unintentional. And yet his unintentional action shattered so much for so many people. I still think about him daily. Something deep within me said, *This is not going to be my story.* I had been on a destructive path, and his passing—and my question—jarred me into choosing a different way.

My second question in the surgeon's office was intentional: I wanted to do whatever I could do to get better. I no longer just wanted to remove the pain, regardless of the cost. I was resolved to *live*. What I thought was the end of my journey was simply a crossroads—and a new question had opened up a new path.

That pivotal question, *Is there anything else out there that can help me with what I'm currently experiencing—and if so, where can I find it?*, led me to additional questions. The most important one was "Despite my current condition, what is the best thing I can do right now to support myself?" To this day, I ask that question over and over again, each day . . . many times. And when I answer it, I take action: I drink a glass of water. I take a breath. I go home early. I stretch. I call a friend. I rest—whenever, wherever. Right away.

And this question has morphed into various forms: How can I best adjust my environment to better support my needs? Who can I find to teach me what I need to know? What small steps can I take each day to build my resilience? What can I do to help others?

These core questions don't change, but the answers do. Gradually I have come to understand what I need and what I can do to care for myself in each moment—and how my body and mind can grow stronger through small, daily steps.

These generative, reflective questions, repeated over and over and faced head-on, have led me to hundreds of small, immediate, intentional changes that have reshaped my life in ways I didn't imagine were possible. Along the way, I was diagnosed with Ehlers-Danlos Syndrome (a complex genetic disorder that affects connective tissues) and multiple other comorbidities. Finally, I had names for my experiences. It wasn't all in my head. It was real.

I still have pain, and persistent, profound health situations, but no longer do they spiral out of control, no longer do they consume me and obscure the beauty and possibility and gratitude that fill my life. The sheer act of asking intentional, healing questions activated the better parts of me, the curious me, the searching me, the courageous me, and they started me down a path of dignity and discovery.

We all have a deep need to be seen and heard, particularly those of us with serious and sometimes debilitating chronic illnesses. Our diseases distract us, define us, and separate us from others—and ourselves, if we let them. A path forward is to begin asking ourselves powerful questions that allow us to take care of ourselves in the ways we need, to see ourselves in new ways. For if we want others to see and hear us, we first need to see and hear ourselves, and most of us don't truly know ourselves and don't understand the complexities of who we are or see the amazing potential within us.

Acknowledgment and celebration are foreign to most of us. Self-acknowledgment and self-celebration are even more foreign. My hope is that these questions will not only allow you to recognize and celebrate your resilience, but lead you down a new path toward meaning, purpose, growth, and fulfillment—whatever your health situation may be.

## THE POWER OF QUESTIONING

I (Gregory) met Brianna at an online networking event in the early days of COVID-19 while figuring out how best to use my questions online in small Zoom breakout groups to generate the openness, authenticity, and vulnerability we so needed then to seed relationship building, reduce social isolation, and deepen friendships. The methodology worked well, and reliably led to powerful, vulnerable sharing. Brianna was in one of my breakout groups, and I soon realized that she not only was passionate about questioning, but had triumphed over painful challenges that would have crumpled me. I wanted to get to know her and learn more about what she'd been through and how she had managed it. The more we spoke, the more I was moved by what she shared with me, and we resolved to work together to create this book as a tool for discovery, personal growth, connection, and understanding for those grappling with the realities of living with serious chronic disease.

Our audience is broader than that, though, because the painful experiences she and others with chronic illnesses endure arise from the many less intense or less relentless pains that so many of us face at one point or another. We all could benefit from vicariously grappling with dilemmas and questions associated with chronic illness; as besides helping us understand and empathize, they provide perspective on our own struggles.

Through our many conversations about the questions we were developing, and the countless stories they evoked about the courageous, painful, resilient journey she and others with chronic debilitating conditions are on, we came to see something inspiring and unexpected. The practices Brianna had developed in her daily grappling with the extraordinary emotional and physical pains and demands of her condition, both before and after its diagnosis—practices of small, intentional daily steps towards positive change and growth, fueled by repeated celebrations of every small daily win along the way—could be combined with the questions about meaning, purpose, beliefs, aspirations, and values that I'd been refining for forty years. Together, they could offer a nurturing, healing new path forward for us all.

## Some Background

I first began to think about a Book of Questions in 1984, when the power of questioning was very underappreciated, and the idea of a book with only questions was so novel that it seemed absurd to most people. How could that be a book? Why ask questions and not guide people towards the "right" answers? Why not analyze people's answers and tell them what their answers revealed about them? My response was that the questions I'd crafted and been using widely worked so well because they surfaced tensions between contradictory values and beliefs, projected us into dilemmas with no easy answers, or evoked memories of powerful moments in our lives. Setting them in isolation empowered them. The blank space around them shouted that this was *not* some quiz but an invitation to explore. People's answers mattered, of course, but what mattered more was the process of embracing the dilemmas, finding those answers, going wherever they led, and sharing responses authentically and vulnerably.

I had crafted my first of these questions a year earlier, after a weekend retreat in Breitenbush, Oregon, where I found myself with a half-dozen others one evening in an unpredictable, careening, intoxicating conversation that lasted until dawn. It was exhilarating because it was so probing, open, honest, and even playful. It saddened me the next day to realize that I hadn't had such a conversation for years. When would it happen again? There had to be some way, I thought, to reliably create that kind of interaction. Could the right questions posed in the right way work? Maybe.

The next day, I crafted a few with a friend. The first one was: "If you saw someone in a café and knew that if you went over and spoke, the two of you would fall completely in love, but you also knew that in six months they'd get hit by a bus and die—would you walk away or go over, assuming you'd forget your fate once you did?"

Not a surprising first question, perhaps, as I was recently divorced and searching for love. The questions led to such powerful conversations that I used them everywhere, refining them, perfecting them, creating more. They were my major preoccupation for a year before the idea emerged to self-publish them into *The Book of Questions*, which went on to become a #1 *New York Times* bestseller that was translated into 35 languages after it was picked up by Workman Press.

How different it was then. Ronald Reagan and Mikhail Gorbachev were in office. The Berlin Wall was standing. Prozac had just been released. Bruce Springsteen's "Tunnel of Love" topped the charts. Digital cameras, the Web, and the Human Genome Project didn't exist. A good mobile phone cost $2,500, weighed two pounds, and had to be charged after an hour of talking at 50 cents a minute. Social media didn't exist, and Brianna hadn't been born.

Yes, everything was different, and yet nothing was different. People struggled then as they do now with money and family, love and loss, hope and fear. They grappled with illness, death, failure, and frustration. They sought meaning, purpose, fulfillment. They knew temptation and betrayal. They struggled, as we do, to carve a place in the world and to understand themselves and others.

The heart of humanity hasn't changed, but culture and technology have. And our understanding of questioning has dramatically advanced as well. Today, the idea of a collection of questions is mainstream, progressing from something I stumbled upon as a potent tool for interpersonal engagement into a new genre: the question books and decks we see today.

## The Field of Questioning

The power of questioning now is harnessed in many settings: In 1986, David Cooperrider and Suresh Srivastva at Case Western Reserve University founded the field of Appreciative Inquiry, a methodology whereby businesses facing challenges use open-ended questions to dig into what is right about their organizations, rather than what problems need fixing. Arthur Aron, at SUNY Stony Brook, used 22 of my questions from The Book of Questions to anchor his Fast Friends technique to engineer interpersonal closeness.[1] He found that a mere 45 minutes of paired engagement around these questions would lead on average to deeper feelings of closeness than a third of people feel when they think of their best friend in life. In 2021, Nicholas

---

[1] Arthur Aron et al., "The Experimental Generation of Interpersonal Closeness: A Procedure and Some Preliminary Findings," *Personality and Social Psychology Bulletin* 23, no. 4 (1997), 363–377. He later popularized these questions in the widely cited feature article "The 36 Questions That Lead to Love" by Daniel Jones in *The New York Times*, January 9, 2015.

Epley at the University of Chicago showed that, contrary to people's expectations, conversations driven by deep, open-ended questions were no more awkward than those spawned by the more mundane fare that is more common.[2]

It is now well understood that these sorts of open-ended questions have major beneficial effects in ways that extend even beyond facilitating intimacy and understanding. They enhance learning by helping us dig more actively and deeply into new ideas and concepts. They evoke personal growth by leading us to introspection and new ways of thinking. They enhance well-being by clarifying our hopes and fears and needs in healthcare settings. And when discussed in the small groups that are natural to us as social primates, they can bring the release of the hormone oxytocin, which occurs when we hug someone or feel understood.

---

[2] Nicholas Epley et al., "A Prosociality Paradox: How Miscalibrated Social Cognition Creates a Misplaced Barrier to Prosocial Action," *Current Directions in Psychological Science* 32, no. 1 (2023), 33–41.

Oxytocin makes us feel socially connected and safe, mediates pair bonding, and reinforces affiliative behavior.[3]

Strong social connection powered by feelings of belonging has been so critical to human survival that we cannot escape its pull. Being isolated and alone was an existential threat for our distant ancestors, and social isolation now is associated with poor health, depression, loneliness, reduced life expectancy, and a host of other psychological problems. The need for connection and for social and emotional support is particularly strong for those dealing with difficult chronic illnesses that can be so socially isolating.

Relationships are built on two pillars—stories about who we are, and questioning that brings out those stories and leads us to probe

---

[3] T. M. Love, "Oxytocin, Motivation and the Role of Dopamine," *Pharmacol. Biochem. Behav.* 119 (2014), 49–60.

new terrain, see ourselves and others in new ways, and deepen connection and intimacy. It is ironic that we often try so hard to show, and even exaggerate, our strengths, hoping they will make people like us, when what most builds trust and friendship is honest self-disclosure that reveals our vulnerabilities. The right questions posed in the right way with the right people in situations that support trust and authenticity can be transformational.

Engaging with the questions here provide a way to be seen and heard—something we all need, but particularly those struggling with chronic, often debilitating conditions.

## THE CHRONIC ILLNESS JOURNEY

There are many demands on our attention today; everyone seems to be competing to sell us something, tell us something, show us something. And many of the online digital assaults are designed to be addictive. The Book of Questions series invites you to stop for a moment, look into yourself, reflect on things you may not have considered before, listen to others, and embark on explorations into what you really care about, who you really are, what you really are seeking, what you are afraid of, what you are inspired by, and so much more.

*The Book of Questions: Living with Chronic Illness* focuses on how life is experienced by those with a chronic disease: how it differs from and is similar to life without that challenge. It's a tool to help those suffering open up to issues they might otherwise ignore, and to do so not only with others facing similar struggles, but with caregivers, friends, and family who want to understand them in a deeper way but don't have the tools to get past the awkwardness.

Too often, those with chronic conditions are not seen, nor heard, nor understood. Too often, they (like everyone) shy away from the difficult topics that need exploration. Too often they miss the humor and the strangeness of their journeys. In dealing with chronic illness, they typically don't get solutions to their problems or answers to their questions. They struggle to explain to others what's going on with them. Doctors don't have answers for them. And all of it can create confusion and isolation in their day-to-day existence.

This book emerged from a year of conversations we (Brianna and Gregory) had about the dilemmas, conflicts, and values that we too rarely face and discuss, particularly when they involve the tensions that arise between those living with a chronic illness and those who support and care for them.

## HOW TO USE THIS BOOK

If you have a chronic illness, this book is an invitation to carve out safe places to hear and see yourself. To look within for the answers. To explore new situations, dilemmas, and concepts in useful ways.

But it is much more than that. At the beginning of this introduction, Brianna shared some simple questions she returns to again and again. These questions have now evolved into a daily practice:

- Despite how I'm feeling in this exact moment, what can I do to best support myself starting now?
- What are the tools and resources that best support me in my times of need, and where can I put them so they'll be accessible when I need them?

- In the challenges I'm experiencing right now, what's one thing I can celebrate about my own resilience?
- How can I support someone else today?

Answering and acting upon these questions each day will change your life, as the small individual steps accumulate and compound in transformative ways. We've repeated these 4 Daily Questions at the end of the introduction for easy reference.

Finding answers to these simple questions is not easy, though. How can we best support ourselves? To know how to answer, we must know ourselves. And that's where the rest of this book comes in.

The 111 questions in this book can help you see, hear, and know yourself better. You can answer them in order at your own pace, flip through the book and find ones that speak to you, or just open to random pages.

You can use these questions in two distinct ways. First, you can answer them for yourself, in your mind or in a journal, perhaps at regular intervals as a personal practice. (*The Book of Questions: Living with Chronic Illness Companion Journal* was designed to support this kind of practice.) This process of responding to the questions to better know yourself, and then returning to the 4 Daily Questions, empowers you to create your unique path of growth and fulfillment, whatever your symptoms or prognosis may be.

Second, you can share your answers with others. But if this is the first time you've found the courage to share your suffering with others, it's important to choose the right person. Though it's natural to want to share with someone close to you—a partner, parent, child, or best friend—we'd like to gently suggest that the best person to be vulnerable with initially is probably not them. As much as they care about you, it may be difficult for them to hear your honest answers about your pain and suffering without distancing themselves or getting defensive, especially with issues that involve them personally . . . and it may be harder for you to be honest with them than you think.

Instead, we recommend reaching out to someone with a chronic illness adjacent to yours. Why not the same illness? Because sharing your most vulnerable experiences with someone who has the same condition as you can often invite comparison, which can get in the way of connection. Someone with symptoms that are similar but not identical to yours can relate with your experience just enough to truly see and hear you. They don't have an ongoing relationship with you and aren't as affected by what you think and do. They are free to be a compassionate witness.

Moreover, these successful conversations will build your strength for more difficult conversations when they occur. As you grow more comfortable with sharing openly, it will feel safer to share with those closest to you.

As you use this book, you'll see that the questions jump from subject to subject, so that if you read them in order (but hopefully not all at once!), you'll still face unexpected issues and topics. Notice those you're drawn to and those you shy away from, as we react to questions that touch unresolved issues for us. Questions you shy away from may be the very ones you most need to focus on.

There are no right or wrong answers to these questions. Answering them authentically is a gift not only to others, but to yourself, as the answers may surprise you and provide grounding and clarity that anchors you. So, let yourself be swept up in these situations. Make yourself care about the choices you make, even when they are hypothetical. And resist the temptation to escape dilemmas by denying their reality or by finding complications to obscure them.

Push beyond a simple "yes" or "no." Probe and explain your responses. Look into your heart. Be honest and brave. Let your mind grapple with the difficult choices you find. Voice some of the uncomfortable ideas you usually steer away from—those flitting, provocative thoughts whispered by an inner voice. They may feel awkward or intrusive, but often they're the very thoughts that can open new paths to intimacy and understanding, especially when grappling with issues you really care about.

If you show up with honesty and integrity, these questions will lead you to intriguing, unexpected, rewarding discussions and explorations. Exploring your vulnerable responses to the questions could be the best gift you give yourself—releasing some of the trauma, guilt, and shame from living with chronic illness. You will learn much about yourself, and you may strengthen your resilience and discover strengths you've developed during your journey.

 Throughout the book, you'll see this QR code. If you scan it, you will be able to share your answers to select questions and see how others have answered them.

The more you engage with these questions, the more they will bring you. As you come to understand yourself and find your voice, you will be able to more effectively communicate your experience and your needs to others. And as you discover what you can and cannot change, you will create your own path of acceptance and growth— one question at a time.

# Quick Start Guide

There are two sets of questions in this book: the 4 Daily Questions in the introduction, and the questions in the remainder of the book.

You can use the 4 Daily Questions as a daily practice. Answering and acting upon them each day will change your life, one small step at a time.

The rest of the questions are numbered but need not be answered in order. Choose one question at a time, and answer honestly. You can use them in two ways that sometimes overlap:

1. Answer the questions for yourself, in your mind or in a journal (or even online, using the QR code) at whatever pace feels comfortable, ideally coupled with the 4 Daily Questions. You're committing to getting to know yourself better over time, and empowering yourself with that knowledge on a daily basis.

2. Share your answers with someone else. If it's your first time sharing something this vulnerable, consider sharing your answers with someone who has an adjacent chronic illness, to give yourself the very best chance for connection.

# 4 Daily Questions

- Despite how I'm feeling in this exact moment, what can I do to best support myself starting now?

- What are the tools and resources that best support me in my times of need, and where can I put them so they'll be accessible when I need them?

- In the challenges I'm experiencing right now, what's one thing I can celebrate about my own resilience?

- How could I support someone else today?

# THE BOOK OF QUESTIONS

Living with Chronic Illness

*Given that you suffer from a chronic health-related challenge with no immediate end in sight . . .*

**Scan this QR code or visit BOQ.life to share your answers and see how others have answered.**

# 1

Do you focus more on what you've gained as a result of illness and hardship, or on what you've lost?

- How might doing more of the other change your life?

## 2

If you had $25,000 to spend solely on easing the challenges in your life, what would you spend it on and why?

- How much would the change mean to you?

# 3

Has there been a time you felt really hurt by someone who didn't understand your illness? If so, what enabled you to move on?

# 4

Do you lie to your doctors, family, or caregivers about following through with treatments? Why?

- If you could have your doctor accurately monitor all your health-related activities, would you want that?

## 5

Which would you prefer: Traveling back in time to some prior moment in your illness journey and reliving your life illness-free with your current life erased? Waking up tomorrow completely cured? Or moving forward on your current path?

# 6

What health-related weakness do you hide, and why? What do you think would happen if you were completely open about it?

# 7

What valuable empathies or perspectives have your health struggles led you to?

## 8

Is the idea of being with family and friends for a holiday more likely to raise your spirits or evoke anxiety?

# 9

If you could live a month each year in total remission, knowing that afterwards your illness would return in full force, would you, and why?

- If so, would you still make the same choice if you knew your condition would worsen after each remission?

## 10

If you knew that sharing the full story of your health struggles would help others, would you do it?

- Do you think your openness would ultimately enhance or diminish your life, and in what ways?

## 11

Are there moments when you entirely forget your illness? If so, what sparks these moments, and what could you do to have more of them?

## 12

If you were painfully ill and had $2,000,000 to either leave to your family or cure your illness, which would you choose?

- What if you would get only one year of life after the cure?

## 13

If you had six months to live, would you rather know or be spared the knowledge, and why? How do you think your life would be better because of your choice?

## 14

What is something important you've learned about yourself from your health-related struggles?

# 15

If you had modest but adequate finances, would you rather have someone give you $500,000 for your own use, or ten times that to support others with your illness?

■ Would your desire to help others be less if the recipients had a different disease from yours?

## 16

If a cure could be found for your illness by halting medical research on all other diseases for two years and focusing solely on your condition, would you choose that path if it were up to you? If so, how would you justify it?

## 17

During your worst moments, what, if anything, have you been able to feel grateful for, and how, if at all, did those feelings help sustain you?

## 18

Do your feelings of responsibility to others help you through your darkest struggles or add to your burdens? How so?

## 19

Have you recently worried about your health? If so, what worried you most?

## 20

What experiences with your illness have been particularly embarrassing?

- How does looking back on them now feel?

## 21

If you could no longer satisfy your partner sexually, would you rather have them forgo sex or seek sexual gratification with someone else? What do you think would be the long-term consequences of your choice?

## 22

What is the most fulfilling part of your life?

- What do you do to honor and protect it?

*Given that you suffer from a chronic health-related challenge with no immediate end in sight . . .*

**Scan this QR code or visit BOQ.life to share your answers and see how others have answered.**

## 23

What is something in your life that is very confusing to you?

## 24

What sacrifices have you made to afford care, and how has that affected your family dynamics?

# 25

Who witnesses your daily struggles, and how do their attitudes and behaviors make you feel?

▪ Is there anything you could do to shift the dynamic between you to improve your experience with them?

# 26

Who do you think will most miss you when you're gone?

- Have you spoken to them about how your absence might affect them, and if not, is there anything good that you think might come out of having such a conversation with them?

# 27

Beneath your illness identity, who are you?

- What could you do to embrace that part of your identity more fully, and how might doing so enhance your life?

# 28

Do you feel stronger or weaker when you refuse to sacrifice your own health needs in order to fit in?

- Would your life be better if you were more forceful about your needs or less forceful?

## 29

When did you nearly do something very wrong for you, but stop? What happened?

# 30

What stories do you tell yourself about your illness, and what purposes do they serve for you?

■ Are there other stories that might better serve you?

## 31

If a cure for your illness were developed but you had no way of accessing it, would its existence be more of a comfort or a curse?

- To what lengths would you go to gain access to a cure, and what do you think the pursuit might cost you?

## 32

What's the best advice you've gotten about managing your illness, and in what ways did it help you? How—if at all—have you thanked the person who brought you this wisdom, and what would you say to them now if you saw them?

## 33

In what ways—if any—is hope important to you?

- How do you develop and sustain hope despite the challenges of your illness?

## 34

If you were to become hypersensitive to cold, would you move to a warmer climate even if it would burden others?

## 35

What is one of the more emotionally painful things you've been through, and what strength of yours helped you deal with it?

- What did you learn from the experience?

## 36

Do you believe your hardest struggles have increased your resilience and your ability to cope, or weakened them? In what ways?

# 37

What habits or attitudes most define your life?

- Are they more the product of pain and struggle, or something else?

## 38

What have you managed to do that made you proud because you thought you'd never really be able to pull it off?

## 39

What boundaries—if any—have your limitations led you to set for yourself? How well do they work for you, and do you think you might be better served either by strengthening or by relaxing them?

## 40

What insight about your condition has significantly shifted your sense of who you are or aspire to be?

- What good—if any—has come out of that shift?

## 41

What is something health related you feel particularly grateful for, and why?

## 42

What is one of the worst experiences you've had involving your health?

- What good—if any—came out of it?

## 43

What is the best thing about being you?

## 44

What is one of the biggest sacrifices you've made to help someone, and why did you do it?

- In what ways did it ultimately enhance or diminish your life?

## 45

When—if ever—have you felt that people truly understood what you go through with your illness?

- Do you think the best way for people to understand your health struggles would be for them to pay more attention or for you to open up more about what you deal with?

- How would you describe your struggles to someone you really wanted to understand you?

## 46

Do you sometimes use your illness as an excuse to indulge yourself in unhealthy ways, like eating poorly? If so, does it help?

*Given that you suffer from a chronic health-related challenge with no immediate end in sight . . .*

**Scan this QR code or visit BOQ.life to share your answers and see how others have answered.**

## 47

Do you ever feel like a stranger in a strange land? What feels most isolating to you?

# 48

When have you had to ask a stranger for significant help because of your health? Was it hard for you?

- In what ways—if any—did it work out better than you expected?

## 49

Have you ever, as a result of your own suffering, treated someone with great compassion? If so, in what way—if any—did the experience enhance your life?

## 50

What is one of the most uninhibited things you've ever done?

- How do you feel about it looking back?

# 51

Have you ignored your intuition about someone or something health related and later regretted it? If so, what happened?

- Have you ever followed your intuition despite significant pushback from others and were glad you did? If so, what happened?

# 52

What is one of the best qualities of yours forged by your illness?

- Would your family and friends agree?

## 53

Is your desire to have children greater or less because of your illness? Why?

# 54

What are your biggest hopes for the coming year?

- Is there anything more you could do to make them come to pass?

## 55

Does your illness ever make you feel completely out of sync with those around you in situations that seem awkward to leave? If so, can you think of any good way you could leave or be more comfortable?

## 56

Has there ever been a time that you felt grateful for your illness? If so, why?

## 57

Have you ever felt unusually optimistic about your future despite a poor health prognosis? In what ways—if any—did those feelings help you deal with the challenges you faced?

## 58

Have there been times you wished you hadn't been born? If so, what strength of yours got you through those times?

- How else has that strength served you?

## 59

Are there times you've felt truly valued and appreciated without any consideration of your illness? If so, what about you was appreciated, and how did that make you feel?

## 60

If you had an "invisible" illness like chronic fatigue, and someone approached you in a parking lot accusing you of using a fake handicap placard, how would you respond? Why?

## 61

What has been your closest encounter with death, and what is something positive—if anything—that came out of it?

## 62

Do you have a "go-bag," with all the supplies you might need in a health crisis? If so, what is in it, and why? If not, what are five things you'd put in such a bag, and would having them always at hand be comforting?

## 63

If all your disabilities miraculously vanished forever tonight, what big challenges would you face?

## 64

What is the best thing about your illness? The worst thing?

## 65

What have you learned about your illness that really could have helped you if only you'd known it earlier?

- Who might you be able to help by reaching out with that hard-earned knowledge?

## 66

If you accumulated burdensome debt because of your illness, would you declare bankruptcy or try your best to pay it off over time? Why?

# 67

Has anyone ever told you a story about their health struggles that brought you valuable insights about yours? What was it, and how did it help you?

## 68

What—if anything—could you think that would take you just a few minutes and greatly enhance your well-being if you repeated it a few times each day?

## 69

What's the worst advice you've followed about your health? What problems did the advice bring you, and what did you learn from the experience?

## 70

Is your illness the primary focus of your conversations? If so, what sorts of things would you talk about if you never talked about your health issues, and do you think others might prefer that?

## 71

If you had difficulty moving, do you think you'd sometimes stay immobile to hide your dependence on an assistive device?

- Are there similar things that you try to hide, and in what ways do you think this helps you?

*Given that you suffer from a chronic health-related challenge with no immediate end in sight . . .*

**Scan this QR code or visit BOQ.life to share your answers and see how others have answered.**

## 72

What part of your life do you find most satisfying?

# 73

Do you express more gratitude to your family and friends for their sacrifices for you than you'd want to hear from them if your roles were reversed?

- How much do you think it would mean to them if you expressed more appreciation to them?

## 74

What things do you knowingly choose to do that are bad for your long-term health, and what is so important to you about them?

## 75

If you could spend tomorrow afternoon discussing your illness with anyone, whom would you choose, and what would you say?

## 76

Do you feel a sense of camaraderie with those with health challenges like yours, and how much do you value that feeling?

# 77

Has your suffering increased your thirst
for life?

- Do you think you value life more or less than those around you who haven't suffered as much?

# 78

When you tell people how you spend your time, what—if anything—do you hide, and why?

- What positives might come from being more open about those things?

## 79

If you had caring, supportive doctors who didn't understand your condition well enough to provide great care, would you keep seeing them, or discharge them and seek someone else?

## 80

If you had to choose between having friends who completely understand and appreciate you but are rarely around, and friends who don't get you but are nice and regularly present, which would you pick?

## 81

What is something you no longer believe about your illness? What shifted your thinking, and how—if at all—has the change served you?

## 82

When you are swept up in chaos and lose control, how do you stay positive? What is an example of that?

## 83

Do you try harder to resist and defy your prognosis, or to accept and deal with it?

## 84

In what ways—if any—do you use your illness as an excuse to avoid aspects of life that you don't want to face? Do you think you deserve to be applauded for having bravely faced your challenges and pain?

## 85

If you decided to have a child, and you learned that any biological child of yours would face all your health problems, would you be more likely to forgo having a child, seek to adopt one, or just push ahead? Why?

# 86

If you saw a young, healthy-looking person parked in a handicapped spot, getting out of a car without handicap plates, would you say anything, and why?

- What do you think your answer most reveals about you?

## 87

Have you ever been belittled for health-related accommodations you needed? If so, did this enhance your compassion for the suffering of others?

## 88

If you became violently ill in a crowded restaurant and threw up on someone, do you think you'd suffer the shame quietly or open up about your health challenges?

- What would be the long-term difference for you of doing the other?

## 89

If you could trade your illness for a different but similarly severe one, what—if anything—would you pick, and why?

# 90

Have you ever felt truly seen and heard by your loved ones? How much does that matter to you?

- What would (or does) that experience
  feel like?

## 91

Is your resilience something you were born with, or something you developed over time? What, if anything, could you do to make yourself even more resilient, and is that something you'd want?

## 92

If someone you loved wanted to take an amazing monthlong trip that was too strenuous for you, would you encourage them to proceed without you?

- If they started pursuing other activities and you began to feel left out, even though your time together still was as good as ever, would you want them to stop?

## 93

Have you had any meaningful spiritual insights or awakenings because of your illness? If so, what were they, and how has your life changed as a result?

*Given that you suffer from a chronic health-related challenge with no immediate end in sight . . .*

**Scan this QR code or visit BOQ.life to share your answers and see how others have answered.**

## 94

When have you felt at your best in recent years, and why?

## 95

If you felt ill and saw several physicians who told you it was in your head, would you stop looking for treatments and instead seek psychiatric help? Why?

# 96

Are you good to your friends?

- What are the most important things you give them?

## 97

What is the worst pain you've felt? If you could go back in time and watch yourself re-experiencing it, what—if anything—could you whisper to your past self that would be helpful or comforting?

## 98

When have you shown great courage and grit in overcoming something most people take for granted? Did you celebrate your triumph as much as it deserved? How so?

## 99

If you stopped interacting with the people you know who repeatedly diminish you, would it improve your life? What about speaking to them forcefully about stopping the behaviors of theirs that you find painful?

## 100

When someone thinks you're making up symptoms or exaggerating your struggles, do you usually try harder to make them understand, change the subject, or pull away from them? Why?

- What do you think would happen if you did one of the others more often?

## 101

Do you more often underplay your health struggles so as to avoid attention, or talk about them so as to get attention?

## 102

How do you handle people who are always asking how you are feeling and whether you are OK?

- Can you think of better ways of dealing with them?

## 103

If you were dying, would you rather make a farewell video for your loved ones, leave them a note, speak to them directly, or say nothing? Why?

## 104

When have you been angriest at someone for not suffering, not understanding, or not caring, and what triggered those feelings?

## 105

When you see someone who has the same disease symptoms you have, but handles them better than you, do you feel more inspired or diminished?

- Have you ever tried to find someone like this to learn from?
- If so, what did you learn? If not, what held you back?

## 106

If you were a caregiver for someone with difficult health issues, and you could somehow change places with them for a month to understand their lived experience, would you? Why?

## 107

Would you wear sneakers or other casual shoes to a formal event if that was the only way for you to be comfortable?

## 108

How has your illness changed your view of yourself?

- Do you now identify more as someone primarily defined by the illness that afflicts you, or as someone with many facets who also happens to be dealing with your illness?

- How much has this changed for you over time?

## 109

What is the most ambitious vision you've had for yourself?

## 110

If you were at a dinner party and began to feel miserable but weren't in danger, would you ask someone to take you home, or stay and suffer so as not to ruin the evening for others?

- Would there be any value in doing the other more often?

# 111

Where would you place yourself today on a scale from 0 to 10, where 10 is the most honest you've ever been about showing the real you to others?

- What do you imagine your life would be like if you forced yourself to be a 12 on this scale for the next year?

# ACKNOWLEDGMENTS

**FROM BRIANNA:**

My greatest thanks and gratitude go to those who made it possible for me to be alive now—without you this book would never have been undertaken.

Joshua, thank you for being my rock, my support squad leader, and above all else, my inspiration to attempt, explore, push the bounds, and create the life of my dreams despite the daily struggles that I experience while navigating a progressive chronic illness.

Kelly, thank you so much for being the wind beneath my wings, my best friend, and number one cheerleader throughout all of my symptoms. You have been such a source of friendship, support, and compassion in my darkest times. Thank you so much for all the ways that you've shown up for me, including being the catalyst for my diagnosis.

Ana Paula, thank you for who you are, how you show up, and the massive impact you have made on my life and help me make in the world each day. I'm grateful for you and all the projects we embark on—especially this one, which has been so deeply meaningful. Thank you for being there in the hardest of times and for listening and supporting me through all the crazy symptoms I experience in a given week. I love you.

Paula, thank you for being a constant source of goodness my entire life. You were a lifeline in every pivotal moment of my formative years and

I'll forever be grateful. You were the first person to make me feel seen and heard. I have worked tirelessly to do the same for others to ripple your goodness outward.

Dr. Slava, thank you for believing that I could be stronger than I ever thought possible. Thank you for cheering me on and for making sure that every time a new symptom presented itself, you were there with the right tools and strategies. I'm forever grateful that you showed me what an incredible doctor-patient relationship looks like.

Cynthia, thank you for being a thought partner, an incredible mentor, and an amazing friend to help me explore the most complicated questions surrounding these sensitive topics. Thank you for hearing me, thank you for seeing me, and thank you for supporting this body of work.

Scott, thank you for changing the trajectory of my life. Without you, I truly don't know where I'd be. You are the reason I ask intentional questions and will continue to ask intentional questions for the rest of my life.

Brian, thank you for being the spark that ignited my wellness journey. Thank you for believing that I was far stronger than I even imagined and for your patience and encouraging spirit while teaching me to walk again; you truly catalyzed my strength journey.

Carolyn, thank you so much for who you are and how you invite me to shine, even in my darkest moments. I appreciate you beyond words.

Arantxa, thank you so much for your incredible leadership and encouragement throughout the final stages of this project.

Paola, thank you so much for your support in bringing our vision to life!

Greg: Last but not least, thank you for being such an extraordinary mentor, colleague, coauthor, and hero! You have brought out the very best in me and encouraged me every season that we've been on this journey together. I couldn't imagine how different life would be if it weren't for our friendship. You have been the catalyst for unlocking my voice and expanding my potential. Thank you for everything.

## FROM GREG AND BRIANNA:

Thank you, David Homan, for introducing us and making this project possible. You truly are the Master Connector. We are grateful for the chain of connections that led us through you to this very special book of questions and much more.

We also thank Amanda Rooker for her sterling editorial work on the manuscript and her help in shepherding it through this collaborative journey, Katie Carroll for the final polish, and George Stevens for his wonderful design and layout work.

# ABOUT THE AUTHORS

Questions have always been **Dr. Gregory Stock**'s passion. He started asking them as a child and never stopped. His question books are mini-classics that have sold more than 5 million copies and been translated into 25 languages. He has a PhD from Johns Hopkins and an MBA from Harvard, and has written more than 60 papers and three influential books on technology, ethics, and public policy in the life sciences. Greg has spoken at venues ranging from the Royal Society, TED, The Vatican, Microsoft, and the World Future Society to Harvard, Stanford, UCLA, and Princeton, and he has made more than a thousand media appearances to discuss questions, values, and other topics on shows ranging from *Oprah* and *Larry King Live* to *Science Friday*, *Nova*, and *Talk of the Nation*.

Greg has often appeared on TV and radio as an authority on the implications of emerging life-science and medical technologies, and he serves on the California Advisory Committee on Stem Cells and Reproductive Cloning. He is presently an adjunct professor at the Icahn School of Medicine in New York and the Chairman and CEO of Socratic Sciences, where he is working to harness the power of questions to enhance understanding and human connection online at a global scale. He has a daughter, Sadie, who is studying computational neuroscience at the University of Southern California and is a coauthor with him of *The Book of Questions: College and Life*.

Learn more at gregorystock.net and socraticsciences.com.

**B**rianna Greenspan is a resilience strategist, wellness educator, author, and chronic illness advocate who has devoted her life to transforming personal adversity into a mission of service, education, and hope.

Diagnosed with Ehlers-Danlos Syndrome after years of uncertainty and setbacks, Brianna turned her lived experience into a pathway for helping others navigate invisible illnesses with courage and compassion.

Brianna is founder and CEO of BGI International, a culture change organization. BGI partners with schools, healthcare systems, and mission-driven organizations to create environments where well-being, social & emotional learning, and a growth mindset are woven into everyday life.

As a biotech entrepreneur, Brianna has played a key role in advancing awareness of Hereditary alpha tryptasemia (H$\alpha$T), collaborating with leading research institutions to help validate and bring legitimacy to rare and misunderstood conditions. Her work has supported research, advocacy, and patient-centered education that bridge complex science with real-world hope for families searching for answers.

Brianna's mission extends beyond science into practical tools and reflective resources. She is the coauthor of *The Book of Questions: Living with Chronic Illness* with Dr. Gregory Stock, a gentle guide for self-inquiry and emotional clarity for those navigating chronic and invisible health challenges. She has also developed children's books and resilience resources that help young people and families build emotional literacy and self-advocacy skills early on.

At the heart of Brianna's work is her belief in micro-massive action: the small, intentional steps we take each day, even when pain or fear make progress feel impossible. Whether Bri is mentoring young people, connecting medical communities, or speaking on global stages, she lives by her reminder to all who feel unseen: Keep shining. The world needs your light.

www.ingramcontent.com/pod-product-compliance
Lightning Source LLC
Chambersburg PA
CBHW051947290426
44110CB00015B/2142